Child Millionaires

Teaching Kids about Money and Wealth

Table of Contents

Chapter 1. Introduction

In this exciting Special Report, explore "Child Millionaires: Teaching Kids about Money and Wealth." Unravel the secret behind raising financially savvy children who understand the value of wealth and how to create it! With a blend of practical advice, real-world case studies, and ingenious money-making activities for kids, this guide will not only educate but enchant. Dive into a treasure-trove of wealth education specifically curated for the young minds who might just be the budding billionaires of tomorrow. Don't miss this thrilling opportunity to unlock your child's hidden potential and, in the process, create a financially secure future for them. This Special Report is more than just a purchase; it's an investment in your child's prosperous future. Let the journey to financial wisdom begin!

Chapter 2. The Fundamentals of Money and Wealth

Understanding the principles of money and wealth is like learning a new language. It is vital, revolutionary, and, unfortunately for many, a foreign language that seems impenetrable. This needn't be the case. Let's embark on an exciting journey that will drastically redefine your child's perspective on money and wealth.

2.1. Understanding Money

Before we can delve into the complexities of wealth, we must first establish a concrete understanding of money—what it is, its purpose, and how it works.

Money, in its most basic form, is a tool that allows people to trade what they have for what they want. It's a medium of exchange that solves the problems of barter by acting as a universally accepted measure of value. Explain this concept to your child using a simple example. Suppose your child loves apples but only has oranges. In the world without money, he/she would have to find someone who happens to want oranges and has apples—an often difficult and time-consuming task. Money solves this problem by providing a standard value for goods, making exchanges quick and efficient.

2.2. The Different Forms of Money

Money comes in many different shapes and sizes, and it's important to teach your child about these forms and their respective value.

Talk about rare forms of money like commodities (gold, silver), cryptocurrencies, etc.

It's important for your children to understand the transition from traditional forms to digital and virtual currencies. Explain that irrespective of the form, money holds value and serves the same purpose.

2.3. The Value of Money

The elusive concept of 'value' can be difficult for children to grasp. It's paramount to teach them that money isn't just about buying things—it's a representation of value.

For young children, use concrete examples. If your child loves a particular toy that costs $10, teach them to understand that this toy is worth 10 dollars in value. As they grow older, introduce concepts like inflation and deflation—that the value of money itself isn't static and can change over time due to various economic factors.

2.4. Earn, Spend, Save - The Money Cycle

Teaching your children the 'Money Cycle'—earn, spend, save—is a crucial step in their financial education.

Through chores or tasks, let them earn their money. This not only gives them a sense of accomplishment but also teaches them about the effort it takes to earn money.

Introduce them to spending money wisely by involving them in real-world situations. Grocery shopping, for example, is an excellent way to show them the thought that goes into spending money.

Finally, introduce them to the concept of saving money. Start with a piggy bank, and slowly, introduce them to the concept of a savings account. Discuss the idea of interest and how money can grow over time.

2.5. Understanding Wealth

Once your child comprehends the fundamentals of money, it's time to introduce the concept of wealth. Wealth isn't just about having a lot of money; it's about having a lot of valuable assets. Assets could include money, but they could also be property, stocks, bonds, and even experiences or skills that could potentially generate income.

Share stories about successful people who have amassed wealth not just through earning money but also by investing in various assets. Use age-appropriate games to teach your child about investing and understanding how assets can contribute to wealth.

2.6. Building Wealth

Now that your child understands the basics of wealth, it's time to help them explore ways to create it.

Investing is an essential skill in wealth creation. Help your child realize that the money they save, if invested wisely, can grow exponentially over time. Discuss different types of investments—real estate, stocks, bonds, and mutual funds.

Teaching kids about entrepreneurship could also prove beneficial. Encourage them to come up with a simple business idea. The goal here is not to start the next Amazon, but to expose your child to the idea of creating value that others would be willing to pay for.

Financial literacy is a journey, and these steps towards understanding money and wealth are just the beginning. It's a learning process, not just for your child, but for you, too. As you guide your child on the path to financial enlightenment, you may find yourself acquiring new financial insights as well. Every step forward is a step toward empowering your child with the tools and understanding needed to navigate a complex financial world, thereby setting them up for a financially secure future.

Chapter 3. Understanding Financial Concepts: Savings and Investments

We often hear that compounding is the eighth wonder of the world. But what does it mean? Let's look at it through an example for better understanding. Suppose a child invests $100 today in a bank saving account that promises a yearly interest rate of 5%. After one year, the account will hold $105. The magic happens in the second year - the child earns interest not only on the original $100 but also on the $5 earned in the first year. So, by the end of second year, the account holds $110.25. This is the power of compounding - earning interest on interest.

Understanding the concept of compounding helps us appreciate the value of time in the world of investing. The earlier a child starts investing, the greater their wealth will be due to the compounding effect. Encouraging children to start saving and investing early in life can help them build a significant corpus which multiplies as they grow older.

3.1. Walk the Talk: Practical Money Saving Activities for Kids

Hands-on activities are often the best way to learn and remember new concepts. Here are a couple of fun activities to help children understand the concepts of saving and investing.

1. **The "Save, Spend, Share" Game**: For this activity, provide kids with three clear jars labeled 'Save,' 'Spend,' and 'Share.' Every time they receive money - as a gift, allowance, or as earnings from a chore - they divide it into these three jars. The 'Save' jar will be dedicated to

long-term goals like buying a bike, the 'Spend' jar for immediate desires like candies, and the 'Share' jar for charities or helping a friend in need. This activity lays a basic foundation for budgeting and prioritizing spending.

2. Stock Market Simulation: There are multiple online platforms where kids can practice trading stocks with virtual money. This is a safe and fun way to understand how the stock market works. They can research different companies, decide which ones to invest in, and monitor their virtual portfolio over time to understand the ups and downs of the market.

3.2. Revealing Real-world Case Studies: Child Millionaires

Learning from real-life examples can be inspirational and educational. Let's look at two child millionaires who mastered the art of saving and investing at an early age.

1. Warren Buffett: Known as the "Oracle of Omaha," Buffett bought his first stock at age 11. He saved money by delivering newspapers and invested in a farm at age 14. Today, he's one of the richest people on the planet and a poster child for long-term, value-based investing.

2. Richard Sandrak: Known as "Little Hercules," Sandrak earned money as a child actor. With his earnings wisely managed by his parents, he was able to invest in real estate at a very young age.

It's crucial to remind kids that while these child millionaires represent the extreme end of the wealth spectrum, understanding money, saving, and investing wisely can lead to financial security and freedom.

In conclusion, imparting the right financial habits to children at an early age paves the way for a prosperous future. By providing them with a solid foundation in financial literacy, they not only secure their financial future but also acquire excellent life skills. The ability to handle money wisely is a gift that benefits children all through their lives, allowing them to lead a life of economic stability and independence.

Remember, the goal is not just to create child millionaires. It is to create financially aware and responsible kids who understand the value of money, comprehend the potential of savings and investments, and grow up to be financially prudent adults. A true understanding of these concepts is arguably the best investment one can make for their children's future.

Chapter 4. Your Child and Entrepreneurship: Fostering Business Acumen

Contextualizing entrepreneurship is a key to raising kids that appreciate the value of wealth creation early. It's not about having them run a Fortune 500 company before they're sixteen — instead, the goal is introducing concepts of self-made wealth that can be understood and applied. This teaches skills such as innovation, problem-solving, financial literacy, and self-sufficiency.

4.1. The Basics

Involve your child in business discussions and concepts at a simple and relatable level. Use everyday scenarios, such as trips to the grocery store, to discuss concepts such as supply, demand, pricing, and profit. Explain the role of business in society.

4.2. Teaching Money Value

Begin by teaching children the value of money. Identify ways to earn, save, spend wisely, and donate. This can start with pocket money for small jobs around the house, leading to a basic understanding of work = recompense.

4.3. Encouraging Business Ideas

Fuel their ideas by constantly asking, "How can you solve this problem?" or "How could this service be improved?" Encourage them to think of ways they could earn a profit from their solutions.

4.4. The Lemonade Stand Model

When it comes to entrepreneurship instruction for kids, nothing beats the classic lemonade stand. This method offers lessons on supply, demand, cost of goods sold, pricing strategy, customer service, marketing/advertising and profit/loss understanding, all within a fun "game" context.

4.5. Reading Business Books Together

Business books written for children can make complex concepts understandable. Choose books that convey entrepreneurial concepts through entertaining and meaningful stories. Discuss the book's lessons to reinforce their understanding.

4.6. Introducing Risk and Reward

Teach your child that risks are part and parcel of entrepreneurship but are often necessary for reward. This can be done through games involving venture choices and subsequent gains or losses.

4.7. Financial Literacy Through Games

Use board games that encourage financial literacy and entrepreneurship. Games like Monopoly, The Game of Life, or Cashflow 101, can help children learn about assets, liabilities, investment risks and returns, while providing a fun way to learn.

4.8. Utilizing Technology

From coding apps that teach problem-solving, to artificial intelligence kits that help in product creation, technology can provide invaluable entrepreneurial training. Allow children to explore these tools and discuss lessons learned.

4.9. Exploring Kid-friendly Investment Opportunities

Guide your child through real-life investment opportunities suitable for children. Custodial accounts, junior ISAs, and bonds intended for children can be investment starting points.

4.10. Attending Business Workshops for Kids

Consider enrolling your child in workshops/seminars which are tailored for children. They will learn how to develop business ideas, and equally important, they get the chance to engage with like-minded peers.

4.11. Organizing a Pop-Up Shop

Encourage children to sell their own products or secondhand items in a small, temporary pop-up shop. This activity can hone skills in product presentation, customer interaction, pricing strategy, bargaining, and managing money.

Chapter 5. Importance of Failure

Teaching entrepreneurship must include lessons on failure. Every failed attempt is a step closer to success. It's about nurturing resilience, adaptability and persistence.

5.1. Creating Business Plans

Help them develop business plans for their ideas. This exercise allows them to think through every aspect of their proposed business and can be a great way to introduce concepts like marketing, finance, strategy, and operations.

5.2. Real-life Examples

Draw insights from child entrepreneurs who have successfully established their businesses. These real-life entrepreneurs can make the journey relatable and achievable.

5.3. Proactive Support

Lastly, provide consistent reinforcement and a supportive environment for their entrepreneurial journeys. Encourage their curiosity and initiative to experiment, iterate, and take ownership of their ideas.

Chapter 6. Creating A Young Visionary: Learning About Goal Setting

Starting young is the key to nurturing successful individuals who are confident about their financial future. In this age of entrepreneurship and innovation, there's never been a better time to encourage children to set meaningful financial goals and strive to achieve them. From the classic lemonade stand to more complex ventures like budding tech startups, children today are proving that age is just a number when it comes to wealth creation. In this segment, we delve into the art of goal setting, its importance, and how we can engender it in our children.

6.1. Nurturing the Visionary

To cultivate financially savvy children, we must first inspire them to envision their futures. A vision is more than a vague idea or dream; it's a vivid picture of what they want their future to look like. Encourage your children to think freely about their aspirations by weaving stories around their interests and potential, and guide them to imagine these scenarios in great detail. The more detailed their vision, the clearer their goal becomes.

Make it fun and exciting! Use vision boards or arts and crafts activities to stimulate their creativity. The use of visualization techniques can greatly enhance a child's ability to set and track progress towards their financial goals.

6.2. Setting SMART Goals

Every business guru will tell you about SMART goals: Specific,

Measurable, Achievable, Relevant, and Time-bound. Here's how to teach kids to apply these principles:

- Specific: Encourage your child to be clear about what they want. Instead of saying, "I want to save money," they might say, "I want to save $200 to buy the newest gaming console."

- Measurable: Establish how progress will be tracked. With our $200 gaming console example, your child can monitor progress every time they add to their savings.

- Achievable: The goal should be challenging, but realistic. Discuss your child's allowance or income from chores to establish what's feasible.

- Relevant: The goal should matter to them, moving them closer to their vision. There needs to be a sense of passion and purpose in every goal they set.

- Time-bound: Every goal requires a deadline. In this case, your kid might decide to achieve the goal in a year.

This framework not only provides clear milestones but also enables children to celebrate their victories along the way, adding a positive reinforcement to their goal-setting process.

6.3. Dealing With Financial Failures

Failures are inevitable when one ventures into unchartered financial territories. However, these so-called failures can become valuable lessons if handled constructively. They teach children that setback isn't the end but a speed bump on the road to success. As parents, it is our duty to help our children navigate their feelings of defeat, providing a safe environment for them to understand and learn from their failures.

6.4. Real-Life Examples and Case Studies

Let's take learning from the textbooks to real-world applications. Introducing children to young achievers who've created wealth through creativity, innovation, and perseverance could help them relate more to the concept of financial independence. Discussing the success stories of young entrepreneurs, inventors, or artists could inspire and motivate them to follow a similar path.

Alexandra Scott is a perfect example of this. At only four years old, she started a lemonade stand to help fund childhood cancer research. Her endeavor, "Alex's Lemonade Stand Foundation," has since evolved into a national fundraising movement, making her a beacon of young entrepreneurial success.

6.5. Activities Encouraging Goal Setting

Interactive exercises at home can make learning about finance a routine family event. Involve your children in budget-making activities, encourage them to keep a personal accounts diary, or organize a "create-your-own-business" day to stimulate their entrepreneurial spirit.

These activities not only encourage financial awareness but also involve skills like decision making, future forecasting, and most importantly, the art of making, saving, and spending money wisely. Encouraging children to take up these activities could lead to reigniting hobbies that might later translate into wealth generation avenues.

Goal-setting is a life-skill that extends far beyond financial education. It helps children to plan, prioritize, and take ownership of their future. By inculcating this skill early on, we are preparing our kids for a financially secure future where they are not just smart about money but also competent at creating and managing their wealth. When nurtured from a young age, visionary goal-setting can indeed pave the path to future billionaires!

Chapter 7. Smart Spending Habits: Teach Them Early On

Teaching children about fiscal intelligence at an early age lays the foundation for sound wealth management, investment strength, and economic independence as they grow older. A crucial component of this education is a concept that even several adults struggle with: Smart Spending.

Chapter 8. Smart Spending: The Core Concept

Smart spending is about more than just counting pennies and forsaking all material luxuries. Indeed, it's about fiscal responsibility, understanding the difference between needs and wants, and making informed decisions that maximize the value and satisfaction derived from money spent.

Teaching children to spend smart doesn't diminish their life's enjoyment; in fact, it enhances it. By economizing on some things, they free up resources to spend on what truly matters to them. But how do we instill this delicate balance? The answer lies in building a comprehensive understanding of money from a young age, and taking practical steps that enhance children's financial aptitude.

Chapter 9. Make Budgeting an Adventure

You can introduce kids to the concept of budgeting by allowing them to manage a small amount of money, perhaps their weekly pocket money or monthly allowance. Instead of just telling them how to use this money, involve them in the process of planning it.

Start by setting up two core categories: "Needs" and "Wants." "Needs" can include minor but necessary items the child uses regularly, like school supplies. In contrast, "Wants" could be something aspirational that the child has set his heart on, like a special toy or a book. Use this basic budget structure to lead discussions around setting priorities and making decisions, which will give the child a sense of responsibility and empowerment.

A visual chart is an interactive way of tracking weekly spending. Color-coded categories for needs, wants, and savings can make it fun for your child to budget and track their money.

Chapter 10. The Needs versus Wants Debate

Often, children (and adults!) confuse wants with needs, leading to impulsive or unnecessary spending. Encouraging kids to weigh their needs against their wants before making purchases helps develop a discerning mindset.

A helpful exercise involves making two lists for items your child wishes to buy - one for 'needs' and the other for 'wants'. Sometimes, something that appears to be a 'want' can reveal itself to be a 'need' when seen in the light of broader perspectives like long-term value and utility, and vice versa.

Chapter 11. Understanding Opportunity Cost

Opportunity cost is a bedrock concept in developing smart spending habits. The opportunity cost is the cost of forgoing the next best alternative when a decision is made. It gives a clear view of what's being gained and what's being given up in every transaction.

Communicate this concept to your kids using simple examples. For example, if your son spends his pocket money on a new video game, he will no longer have enough money to go to the amusement park with his friends. By deciding one way, he is giving up the opportunity to enjoy the other. These real-world examples at a relatable level would provide an impactful understanding of opportunity cost, which is the groundwork of prudent spending.

Chapter 12. Patronizing Good Value, Not Just Low Cost

It's a common misconception that smart spending merely equates to buying cheap. Instead, smart spending is about understanding the correlation between price and value, and knowing when to spend more. This approach encourages frugality but not at the expense of value.

Price comparisons when shopping can be a fun and enlightening activity. You can teach children to check prices at different stores or websites and read reviews, look out for better deals, discounts, and quality alternatives that may take a little research before deciding on a purchase. This skill will also instill patience in spending habits.

Chapter 13. The Importance of Saving and Giving

Smart spending isn't just restricted to how one spends money, but also how smartly one diverts funds towards saving and giving.

Children can be encouraged to save towards a goal. The achievement of these savings milestones can be celebrated, enhancing their positive association with the act of saving. Similarly, introduce your children to the idea of philanthropy. Helping others with their resources will instill empathy and a sense of social responsibility.

In conclusion, teaching smart spending habits to kids early on can foster a healthy, lifelong relationship with money. This knowledge will empower them to be prudent spenders, efficient savers, thoughtful givers, and confident investors in the years to come, setting them on a pathway to financial success and wealth creation.

Chapter 14. Money Games: Learning through Fun Interactive Activities

When it comes to teaching kids about money, practical experience, much like in the real world, often trumps theoretical knowledge. Playing money-oriented games offer children a fun, engaging avenue to learn about personal finance. Not only can these games impart key financial lessons, but they also teach critical life skills such as resource management, strategic thinking, and decision-making.

Let's embark on a journey through myriad interactive, entertaining, and educational activities that can transform your child's perception of money, while simultaneously cultivating their financial savvy.

14.1. Money Management with Monopoly

This classic board game needs little introduction. Serving as the perfect board game to impart money education, Monopoly helps children understand the intricacies of managing assets, buying properties, paying taxes, and the consequences of going bankrupt. During this engaging activity, children will gain a sense of property valuation, mortgages, and the fundamentals of property investment. The tangible, hands-on experience of handling Monopoly money also reinforces the concept of financial responsibility.

14.2. Grocery Store Role-Play

Turn an everyday activity into a learning playground! Setting up a mock grocery store at home and encouraging children to 'shop' with a limited budget is a fantastic way to introduce them to the idea of budgeting and smart spending. By allowing them to calculate their total expenditure, figure out the change due, and ponder over the best value for money, kids will intuitively grasp essential math skills and the value of a dollar.

14.3. Financial Interactive Apps

As digital natives, children today learn faster on interactive platforms. There are a plethora of financial education apps designed especially for kids, like RoosterMoney, PiggyBot, and Bankaroo. These apps creatively incorporate games and tasks to teach children about saving, investing, and earning. They also offer tangible rewards for completing the tasks, thus teaching children the fundamentals of earning income.

14.4. DIY Piggy Bank

While saving might be the first real interaction children have with money, interacting with it need not be boring. Help your child make a personalized piggy bank and establish the tradition of saving a certain portion of their pocket money each week. By visualizing their savings grow, children will understand that good financial habits, like saving, can yield fruitful results over time.

14.5. "Save, Spend & Share" Jars

While piggy banks teach the virtue of saving, the "Save, Spend & Share" jars system takes it up a notch by teaching budgeting and philanthropy. Get three jars and label them "Save", "Spend" and "Share". Allocate a certain percentage of every dollar your child receives to each jar. This system will teach them to budget their money, plan for future expenses (Save), enjoy the benefits of their money now (Spend), and give to causes that matter to them (Share) thus, contributing to the society.

14.6. Money Math Card Games

Ingraining math skills at an early age is crucial for financial health. Counting money, understanding decimals and calculating percentages are all important for managing personal finances. Simple card adaptions like 'Monetary Memory', where each card contains a money amount and the child needs to match two cards that equal a dollar, will help enhance their calculations.

14.7. Business Board Games for Older Children

When your child reaches a certain age, games such as 'The Game of Life' and 'Cash Flow for Kids' can be excellent tools to teach more complex financial ideas. Designed to simulate real-life financial strategies and situations, these games teach the importance of investing, asset accumulation, passive income, and applying financial foresight.

14.8. Learning through Stock Market Games

As kids mature, stock market games like 'HowTheMarketWorks' offer an excellent platform to teach the fundamentals of investing. Players realize the importance of economic news, bear and bull markets, and company performance. With no real money at stake, it's a risk-free and fun platform to learn about the stock market.

14.9. Junior Entrepreneurship

Another great venture could be encouraging your child to start a small-scale home-based business, such as selling craft items or lemonade. Task them with managing the money earned, calculating profit, and understanding running costs. This hands-on experience will lay a solid foundation in entrepreneurship and help them acquire financial acumen.

Remember, the goal of these games and activities is not only to equip children with financial knowledge, but also to instill good money habits, inspire wise financial decisions, and foster an understanding that money is not an end in itself but a tool that can be used to create a life that they desire. By integrating financial literacy into leisure time, we make learning about money an engaging and exciting experience for them.

Chapter 15. The Power of an Earned Dollar: Valuing Hard Work

One of the most significant life lessons that we often overlook teaching our children is the understanding of money's real value. Not just what money can buy, but the sweat, effort, thought, and time it symbolizes.

15.1. The Real Value of a Dollar

When we talk about the value of a dollar, we don't just mean the market value. It's about the place a dollar holds as a symbol of labor, the representation of hours spent working. Children who can comprehend and appreciate this concept understand that each dollar they possess has someone's hard work and time embedded within it.

Let's break down this concept further. Suppose your child earns ten dollars for an hour of lawn mowing. It can be explained that this ten-dollar bill encapsulates that one hour of energy, sweat, and sustained effort. So, when your child decides to spend this ten-dollar bill on a toy, they are essentially trading an hour of their work for that toy.

When this perspective is ingrained in the child's mind, the value they place on money transforms dramatically. Suddenly, smart spending and saving hold much more significance – because they are not only preserving dollars but valuations of their precious time and hard work.

15.2. Monetary Compensation and the Theory of Work

It's important to frame your child's understanding of the link between work and monetary compensation early on. Working in this context is not confined to physical labor; it can also mean providing a service, like tutoring, or creating a product, like handmade bracelets.

Let's take, for instance, a lemonade stand. Run a hypothetical scenario with your child where they sell lemonade for a day. Assist them in understanding the different aspects involved - cost of the ingredients, time and effort spent in making and selling the lemonade, and the joy or satisfaction it brings to the customers. Explain how customers pay for the overall experience and not just the lemonade.

This exercise helps children to value the work they do and appreciate that the money earned is a direct compensation for their time, effort, and service provided. Such an understanding further encourages them to improve their offerings to increase their earnings.

15.3. Encouraging Entrepreneurial Initiatives

Promoting entrepreneurial activities is an exceptional way to deepen your child's understanding of the work-money correlation. Such activities can range from starting a small pet-sitting service to creating and selling art or crafts. Encourage your child to keep track of the time invested in these activities, calculate the expenses, and determine how to price their goods or services to make a profit.

Another essential lesson learned in this process is the concept of investment and why it is clever to sometimes wait and grow assets rather than consuming them right away. Discuss how putting effort into their ventures today—whether it's sourcing materials for their crafts or learning and teaching a new skill—can result in greater profits in the future.

15.4. Observing Money Management in Real Life

Real-world observations are key to instilling an appreciation for the process of earning money. If appropriate, share with your child some basics about your work: What you do, how you provide a service or product people are willing to pay for, and the time you dedicate to your job. Use bills, grocery expenses, and other regular costs as concrete examples of how the money you earn gets allocated and spent.

For a more hands-on approach, take them along for shopping trips and explain your purchasing decisions, illustrating how you prioritize needs over wants. Also, involve them in conversations about saving for the future, be it for their college fund, family vacations, or even retirement. This reinforces the message that not every earned dollar is meant to be spent immediately.

15.5. The Interplay of Charity and Gratitude

In discussions about earning money, don't miss the opportunity to introduce the values of charity and gratitude. Encourage your child to allocate a portion of their earnings for a cause they care about. This can be an animal shelter, a children's hospital, or any other charitable organization.

Help them understand that the ability to earn and spend money is a blessing that not everyone enjoys. Those more fortunate have a responsibility to help others.

Moreover, talk about how charitable giving can provide a sense of satisfaction that is a form of income itself. This non-material return on investment is sometimes far more valuable than material gain and breaks down the idea that the goal of earning money is merely to accumulate wealth.

15.5.1. Multifaceted Importance of Hard Work

Teaching a child about valuing hard work is not just about dollars and cents. It's equally about nurturing dedication, resilience, patience, discipline and the ability to delay gratification. These virtues are as valuable as any currency and will hold them in good stead in every phase of life, extending well beyond just money matters. This life wisdom is perhaps the greatest wealth children can inherit from their parents.

In conclusion, preparing your child for a financially secure future doesn't just mean teaching them about making money. It's equally critical to ingrain in them the earnest value that's represented within every dollar earned. This knowledge will not just inform their future economic decisions, but will also shape their character and mindset towards work, money, and life.

Chapter 16. Investing in Their Future: Introduction to Financial Markets

We are all aware that grown-up money matters can seem intimidating and complex, but with the right approach, children can be initiated into the fascinating world of finance. Nowhere is this truer than with the financial markets, a marketplace for the buying and selling financial assets which ensures the smooth functioning of a capitalist economy. This chapter will incubate your children's understanding of financial markets starting from the basics, moving on to how they operate, and finally exploring a few safe ways they could get their hands wet if they wish to.

16.1. What are Financial Markets?

At its most elementary, a financial market is the broad term for any marketplace where buyers and sellers participate in the trade of assets such as equities, bonds, currencies, and derivatives. They are characterized by transparent pricing, strict regulations, costs of 0% to low percent, and the ability to buy/sell at any time as long as the market is open. Financial markets can be found in nearly every nation around the globe.

On the face of it, financial markets provide a forum in which participants like investors and traders can agree on prices for specific financial assets. These markets are essential for an economy to function because they allow money to flow from those who have it (investors), to those who need it (companies and governments).

16.2. Understanding Different Types of Financial Markets

For those new to the world of finance, it can be overwhelming to understand the range of financial markets. Broadly, these markets can be categorized as follows:

1. The Stock Market: This is where shares of publicly traded companies are bought and sold. It's a place where the company can raise capital to expand its business and investors can become part-owners of a company.

2. The Bond Market: This is where borrowers issue debt in the form of bonds, to lenders in the market, usually to raise capital. Governments often use bond markets to secure funding, while investors buy into these bonds as they typically offer stable returns.

3. The Commodities Market: This market deals in raw or primary products, like gold, oil, coffee beans and many more. Here, buyers and sellers trade commodities on the present or future delivery.

4. The Foreign Exchange Market (Forex): This is the world's largest financial market where people can trade currencies. From banks to businesses to currency traders, forex is vital in running the global economy.

5. Derivatives Market: This market trades in contracts that derive their value from underlying assets. For example, options are a popular type of derivative security.

6. Money Market: It's where financial instruments with high liquidity and short maturities - usually under a year - are traded. It's used by participants as a means for borrowing and lending in the short term, with securities that commonly include Treasury bills and commercial paper.

16.3. Decoding Market Operations

Understanding how these financial markets work may seem like a herculean task due to their apparent complexity. But, simplified, the functioning of these markets revolves around a basic demand-supply concept.

Every market has two sides - buyers and sellers. Buyers offer a "bid," or the highest amount they're willing to pay, which is usually lower than the amount sellers "ask," or the lowest amount they're willing to accept. This difference between bid and ask price is known as the spread. A trade happens when the buyer increases their bid, the seller lowers their asking price, or both.

In the operation of these markets, brokers play a crucial role as intermediaries. They connect buyers and sellers and manage the transactions for a commission or fee.

An important concept here is that of market orders and limit orders. A market order is when the buyer or seller asks the broker to execute the trade at the current market price, while a limit order asks the broker to execute the trade at a specific price or better.

Different markets operate at different hours, and this should definitely be kept in mind when participating. Trading schedules are particularly important in the Forex market, which operates 24 hours a day but only for five days a week.

16.4. A Primer on Securities

Securities, or financial instruments, are the assets bought and sold in financial markets. These can be divided into two main types - equity and debt.

1. Equity Securities: The most common form of equity security is stocks or shares. When your child buys a stock, they essentially

buy a piece of ownership in the company. If the company does well, the price of the stock goes up and your kid could sell it for a profit. However, if the company doesn't fare well, the worth of the stock goes down.

2. Debt Securities: These are essentially loans, with the most popular type being bonds. When your child buys a bond, they are lending money to the government or a company. In return, they receive periodic interest until the bond matures, at which point the amount they loaned - the principal - is given back.

Each type of security carries its own risks and rewards, and diversifying - owning a mix of different types of securities - is a common way to manage risk.

16.5. The Role of Regulatory Bodies

Financial markets are supervised by government-appointed regulatory bodies to ensure fair practices and prevent fraudulent activities. For example, in the United States, the Securities and Exchange Commission (SEC) oversees most financial market activities. Transparency and accountability are promoted in the marketplace, helping to build trust and protect investors.

Next, we will embark on the journey of taking these vibrant cognitive illustrations from the realm of theme parks of finance to a more real, near home scenario, where young minds can dip their toes into these treasury pools safely and wisely.

16.6. Introduction to Safe and Smart Investing for Kids

Now, it's time to apply this knowledge. It's essential to remember that investing, in actuality, is about making money grow and not simply gambling on stocks.

Here's a simplified 5-step process to introduce your kids to investing:

1. Set a Goal: Ask your kid to set a financial goal, like buying a new bike or even saving for college. This gives a purpose to their investing journey.

2. Save Money: Encourage them to start saving money towards their goal. This could include setting aside a portion of their allowance or doing small jobs for friends and family.

3. Open an Account: Once they've saved, use a custodial brokerage account - where an adult maintains control until the child reaches a certain age - to start purchasing financial assets like stocks.

4. Understand Risk: Discuss the concept of risk so they understand that the value of their investments will have ups and downs, but the idea is to increase value in the long term.

5. Study and Invest: Teach them to research before investing. Maybe they like a particular clothing brand or tech company. Encourage them to look at these companies' performance before deciding if it's a good investment.

By investing small amounts, kids can learn valuable lessons without risking serious financial loss. They will experience market cycles, learn to read financial statements, and most importantly, learn the importance of patience and discipline in investing. They'll see that investing is a long-term journey, not a quick sprint.

This chapter serves to launch your children onto an exciting journey of financial education and literacy. The world of financial markets is an essential part of that journey. Understanding financial markets could spark an interest in economics, business, or finance. Most importantly, even though it may take time and patience, this journey can equip them with the tools to secure their financial future.

Chapter 17. Leading by Example: The Role of Parents in Shaping Financial Behavior

The crucial path to raising financially savvy children starts at home. Before kids jump into the complexities of budgeting, investing, or bargaining, they grasp their earliest lessons from observing the financial behaviors of adults around them, particularly their parents. It's analogous to how baby birds learn to fly - they watch their parents, then spread their wings and give it a try. The young are keen observers, watching every move and incorporating those experiences into their life model.

17.1. The Role Model in the Mirror

Your own habits, the way you handle money, and how you express your sentiments towards it greatly form the financial cognitive map for your offspring. Your child watches when you haggle at the flea market, when you fret over unpaid bills, when you plan your budget, and even when you splurge on your desires.

Let's express this with the analogy of a mirror. The mirror always reflects the person standing in front of it. The child, in this case, is the mirror, mirroring the parent's financial behaviors and attitudes.

So the question emerges: what are you reflecting to your child?

17.2. Financial Attitude: More Than Just Money

Children perceive money through how their parents handle it, and how they view it. If parents treat finances as a source of stress or conflict, children can acquire those same sentiments. Therefore, it's crucial to realize that your financial attitudes can indirectly shape your child's future financial health.

For example, showcasing frugal behaviors like reusing, recycling, or repairing things instead of throwing them away can instill the value of resourcefulness. In contrast, constantly worrying about money may inadvertently teach kids that money is a source of fear, stress, and instability.

17.3. Building Early Financial Habits

As the saying goes, "Early to bed and early to rise, makes a man healthy, wealthy, and wise." The same applies to financial habits. Teaching them to save, spend consciously, and give jovially at an early age—and leading by example—shapes the pillars of their financial behavior later in adulthood.

Habits such as regular saving, timely returns of borrowed items, conscious purchasing, and prudent resource usage will be cemented into their daily routine, ultimately morphing into characteristics of their personality.

17.4. The Piggy Bank Theory

A brilliant hands-on experience to build early financial habits is through the traditional 'Piggy Bank'. Give your child a piggy bank, along with a small amount of spending allowance. Encourage them to save their pennies regularly, reminding them that those pennies will eventually add up to buy something they desire. This teaches children the virtues of patience, discipline, and delayed gratification.

By contributing their savings towards a purchase, children understand the concept of 'money earned = goods obtained', thereby fostering a sense of achievement and understanding about the value of money.

17.5. Open Discussions on Finance

One key element in leading by example is encouraging open dialogue about money matters. Ensure that your child is aware that discussing money is not taboo.

Engage them in friendly discussions about household bills, expenses, the importance of avoiding debt, and why saving for emergencies or long-term goals is vital. This fosters transparency in financial matters and reinforces the belief that finance is an essential part of life to be contemplated and comprehended, rather than feared.

17.6. Walk The Talk

Children are less likely to do what we merely say, rather, they are more motivated by watching what we do. Are you a prudent spender, a careful budgeter, a disciplined saver? Your children notice it. Conversely, do you spend impulsively, always upgrading to the latest trends or showing disdain towards money? They'll observe that too.

Hence, walking the talk in financial matters not only enhances your financial health but also imparts the best financial lessons to your children.

17.7. Learning from Mistakes: A Step Towards Financial Wisdom

Financial errors are inevitable. The key is not in entirely avoiding these mistakes, but in learning from them. By sharing your financial blunders and recoveries with your children, they understand that errors are part of the journey towards financial wisdom.

This approach also ensures that children don't fear financial mistakes but see them as lessons and opportunities for improvement.

17.8. Conclusion

Inculcating financial wisdom in children is akin to planting a sapling. You plant the seed, water it, provide it light, and remove the weeds around it. Gradually, the sapling turns into a fruit-giving tree, standing tall and strong.

Likewise, steady financial teachings, peppered with life-long lessons and hands-on experiences, mold the child's financial behavior. Such a child, or rather, the young adult now, not only becomes financially competent but also imparts these virtues to subsequent generations, thereby contributing to the financial health and prosperity of the society.

Remember, the journey of a thousand miles begins with one step. Begin the important journey of financial literacy for your children by leading with example today, for the path you traverse today, is the path they are likely to tread tomorrow!

Chapter 18. Mapping the Journey: A Financial Milestone Tracker for Your Child

To create a reliable roadmap for teaching kids about wealth, it's crucial to align their financial education with their age. Here, we present a step-by-step guide that summarizes the financial knowledge and skills kids should have at various ages. It's like a developmental milestone tracker, but for your child's financial knowledge. From preschoolers learning about the importance of money to teenagers earning their keep, this guide challenges us to reflect on what money skills we expect our kids to master.

18.1. The Very Beginning Stage (ages 3-5)

Introducing kids to money should not be complex. At this age, they should begin to understand the basics, like identifying coins and noting that money can be exchanged for goods.

1. *Recognize Coins and Bills*: Encourage your child to learn the varying physical characteristics between different coins and bills. Use actual money or play money for hands-on learning.

2. *Value of Money*: Teach simple comparisons such as a dime is worth more than a nickel, without delving into their actual values.

3. *Exchanging Money for Goods*: Disguise learning as play with pretend shopping. Show them that when they want something, they have to give money in exchange.

Practical Action: Set up a pretend shop at home. Allow them to pick up an object, and then ask them to give a "coin" in exchange for it.

18.2. Taking Small Steps (ages 6-10)

As your child grows older, they should be equipped with more comprehensive money skills. At this stage, they should understand denominations and simple mathematical operations related to money.

1. *Understand Denominations*: Focus on reinforcing the value of each coin and bill. For example, explain that it takes five 1-dollar bills to equal a 5-dollar bill.

2. *Addition and Subtraction*: Kids should be able to calculate basic sums involving money. This includes finding the total amount of money they have and checking if they have enough to purchase a desired item.

3. *Savings*: Introduce the concept of setting aside money for later use.

Practical Action: Introduce an allowance system and a piggy bank. Guide them to divide the money they receive or earn into portions for saving, spending, and giving.

18.3. The Awakening Stage (ages 11-13)

At this stage, kids should be introduced to the basics of budgeting and understanding the differences between wants and needs. This is also the time where concepts like income, expenses, and saving goals should be taught.

1. *Needs vs Wants*: Discussing the difference between essential and non-essential expenses helps children to make wise decisions

when spending money.

2. *Budgeting*: Encourage them to plan how they will spend their allowance. Help them break down their spending by category, just like in a real-world budget.

3. *Saving Goals*: Promote the habit of saving for less immediate and more expensive goals, emphasizing the satisfaction of delayed gratification.

Practical Action: Guide them to set a saving goal for something they want but can't afford immediately. It could be a game, a toy, or any valuable item they want.

18.4. The Teenage Milestone (ages 14-18)

At this stage, teenagers should be introduced to more complex financial concepts like investment, interest rates, and setting long-term financial goals.

1. *Banking Basics*: Acquaint them with concepts like deposit, withdrawal, minimum balance, and bank statement. Online banking can also be introduced with parental guidance.

2. *Interest and Investment*: Teach the basics of how interest works and introduce simple investment concepts.

3. *Earning Money*: Encourage part-time work to instill a sense of responsibility and understanding of earning money.

Practical Action: Open a savings account in their name, and assist them in managing it. Explain how their money can grow with the right investments.

This journey will differ for everyone, as children's curiosity and capacity to understand these concepts can vary wildly. Although ages are specified, these are merely guidelines—not strict rules. Never underestimate the ability of your child to grasp these concepts ahead of schedule. What's most important is the practice and consistent nurturing of these skills, moving at a pace that suits your child best.